147 PRACTICAL TIPS
for teaching online groups
Essentials of Web-Based Education

by
Donald E. Hanna
Michelle Glowacki-Dudka
Simone Conceição-Runlee

ATWOOD PUBLISHING
Madison, Wisconsin

Atwood Publishing
2710 Atwood Ave.
Madison, WI 53704
888/242-7101
www.atwoodpublishing.com

ISBN 1-891859-34-X

Library of Congress Cataloging-in-Publication Data

Hanna, Donald E., 1947
    147 practical tips for teaching online groups: essentials of Web-based education / by Donald E. Hanna, Michelle Glowacki-Dudka, Simone Conceição-Runlee.
        p. cm.
    Includes bibliographical references.
    1. Internet in education. 2. World Wide Web. 3. Computer-assisted instruction. I. Title: One hundred forty-seven practical tips for teaching online groups. II. Title: Essentials of Web-based education. III. Glowacki-Dudka, Michelle, 1971- IV. Conceição-Runlee, Simone, 1963- V. Title.
LB1044.87 .H35 2000
371.33'44678—dc21   00-061069

Contents

Acknowledgments

We, the authors, would like to thank many individuals who have contributed to our thinking and experiences related to online learning — most especially the students enrolled in the graduate programs in Continuing Education and Curriculum and Instruction at the University of Wisconsin-Madison. Of particular note are Pam, Jennifer, Mike, Jamel, Bruce, and Jessica, who together offered valuable insights as this book was being finalized.

We also extend our appreciation to our colleagues at the University of Wisconsin-Madison and other institutions who provided valuable feedback for this project from conceptualization to completion — especially Alan Knox, Kathleen King, Michael Streibel, and Melanie Agnew. Their advice and counsel were of great benefit as this book was being developed.

Finally, we acknowledge and gratefully appreciate the patience and support provided by our families in undertaking this intensely rewarding but time-demanding project. Thanks to Karna, Marek, and Mark for helping us along this journey.

Don, Shelly, and Simone

Foreword

by Parker J. Palmer

The online teaching and learning environment is a new and largely unexplored "space" for learning. While face-to-face learning environments can at times be mysterious and overwhelming even to the most experienced teachers, the online environment is so new that we can offer very little in the way of time-tested truths and effective practices, or even of consistent observation by those closest to it. But by synthesizing their own experiences and integrating the preliminary findings from recent research, the authors of *147 Practical Tips for Teaching Online Groups* have made a major contribution to the development of online teaching and learning at all educational levels, from K-12 through the university.

This book is a welcome relief from the many voices that have called for technology to replace the art and skill of the teacher, whom we have depended upon since the origins of humankind to elevate and amplify our understanding of nature and of human nature. *147 Tips* is rooted in a philosophy of learning that is based on creating a safe space for learning focused on the needs of the learner — a space that a teacher must structure, hold, and protect. The authors then build the case for using technology to engage learners actively within this space — engage them with the teacher, with each other, and with the subject. The authors' ideas have the potential to create a foundation for effective practice on this new educational frontier.

Parker J. Palmer's most recent books are *The Courage to Teach: Exploring the Inner Landscape of a Teacher's Life* (Jossey-Bass Publishers 1998) and *Let Your Life Speak: Listening for the Voice of Vocation* (Jossey-Bass Publishers 1999).

Preface

A UNIQUE LOOK AT THE AUTHORS

We, the authors of this book, believe that if you, the reader, know who is writing a book or speaking about a topic, you can better understand the positions the writers/speakers take and the underlying perspectives for the ideas and arguments they present. That's why, in this section, we introduce ourselves to you and share our profiles from a fun web site called Kingdomality® (http://www.kingdomality.com), which presents a series of questions and helps you define your personality from a medieval vocational perspective. (Note: Kingdomality® and the Personality Preference Profile® are trademarks of Career Management International®, Inc.)

Although these profiles are clearly approximations of who we are, we can find ourselves and each other in all of the descriptions.

Donald E. Hanna is Professor of Educational Communications for the University of Wisconsin-Extension. He has provided leadership in the implementation of learning technologies at the University of Illinois at Urbana-Champaign, Washington State University, and the University of Wisconsin, and he has also taught in the graduate programs in adult and continuing education at these three universities. He currently teaches graduate courses on the organization of educational technology, continuing and higher education, and organizational change in higher education at the University of Wisconsin-Madison.

Don received his Ph.D. in Adult and Continuing Education from Michigan State University in 1978. His experience in online education began in 1987, when he was the coordinator of an online conference as part of the Kellogg National Leadership

Program. He is the author of numerous articles and book chapters. Most recently he authored and edited *Higher Education in an Era of Digital Competition: Choices and Challenges* (Atwood Publishing 2000). He is also the co-author and editor (with Colin Latchem) of a forthcoming book, *Leadership in Open and Flexible Learning* (Kogan Page Publishers, to be published in 2001).

Don's medieval profile is that of the **Discoverer,** whose characteristics include going where no one else has ever gone before. According to the Kingdomality® indicator, regardless of the number of available natural problems to be solved, it's not unusual for Don to continually challenge himself with new situations or obstacles that he has created. Currently his students are teaching him to sail, and he has undertaken this book, much to his enjoyment. He is an insatiable explorer of people, places, things, and ideas. He thrives on constant change and anything new or different.

On the positive side, Don is creatively rational, as well as open-minded and just. On the negative side, he might be impractical and an indecisive procrastinator.

Don's primary focus for this book has been on the overall organization of technology; how appropriate (and inappropriate) uses of technology contribute to organizational and faculty acceptance or rejection of online technologies and methodologies; and how the effective use of learning technologies can improve learning outcomes.

Michelle Glowacki-Dudka is Coordinator of the Wisconsin Statewide Family Literacy Initiative, in association with the Wisconsin Technical College System Board. She received her doctorate in Adult and Continuing Education from the University of Wisconsin-Madison in 1999. Her research has focused on interorganizational collaboration among the public, private, and nonprofit sectors for developing educational programs.

Michelle has multiple interests in organizational development through collaboration, community dialogue, the use of technology in support of learners' needs, and the role of adult educators within higher education. Along with coordinating family literacy programs in the state, she is the co-chair of the Midwest Research to Practice Conference (2000). She has also team taught graduate courses in continuing and higher education that incorporate the web and computer conferencing. She will teach at the University of Wisconsin-Milwaukee in Fall 2000.

Michelle's medieval profile is that of the **Dreamer-Minstrel,** a role also found in most of the thriving kingdoms of medieval times.

Michelle can always see the "silver lining" to every dark and dreary cloud. She excels at viewing the bright side of every situation and understanding why everything happens for the best. Michelle is the positive optimist of the world who provides hope for all humankind — and, more specifically, for Don and Simone. She communicates a terrific enthusiasm for this project to her colleagues. Since Don and Simone have known Michelle, there has never been an occasion so terrible that she did not find some good within it.

On the positive side, Michelle is spontaneous, charismatic, idealistic, and empathic. On the negative side, she may be a sentimental dreamer who is emotionally impractical.

Michelle's primary focus for this book has been on finding concrete connections between philosophy and practice in the implementation of online learning environments. She has concentrated on coordinating the development of the big picture of online learning. She has also shepherded the many details of this project.

Simone Conceição-Runlee is an Instructional Design/Technology Consultant for the University of Wisconsin-Milwaukee School of Education. Her research interests include distance education, educational technology, instructional design, staff development, and adult learning. Her experience involves designing web-based courses for instruction and coordinating staff development activities for faculty and staff.

Simone holds a Master of Science degree in Adult and Continuing Education from the University of Wisconsin-Milwaukee, and she is currently pursuing her doctorate at the University of Wisconsin-Madison in the area of adult and distance learning. Her dissertation focus is on the experiences of college faculty who teach online.

Simone's medieval profile is that of the **Benevolent Ruler,** a role for which she is genuinely loved by her colleagues and friends because of her genuine concern for others. Without her this book would not have been completed, sayeth Don and Michelle. Simone is the idealistic social dreamer of the group, and she does her best to solve the people problems of the world. She is the social reformer who wants everyone to be happy in an online world that you can almost visualize. Above all, she is exceptionally perceptive about the woes and needs of humankind — especially those of online teachers and learners. She often exhibits the understanding and skill to readily conceive and implement solutions that meet others' needs.

On the positive side, Simone is creatively suggestive, charismatic, and ideologically concerned. On the negative side, she may be unrealistically sentimental, scattered, impulsive, and deviously persuasive.

Simone's focus for this book has been to address issues of faculty development from the perspective of good teaching and instructional design, with a special emphasis on meeting learners' needs in the online environment. She has also researched and contributed many aspects of good practice in online environments, and she is an expert in helping faculty understand online and web-based technology tools, software, and design processes.

So, that's who we are. And now, on to the reason for our collaboration — this book!

WHY THIS BOOK?

Online learning is in its infancy. Just as the development of the book extended the range of learning worldwide a few hundred years ago, the World Wide Web has recently enabled knowledge resources to be accessible in ways that were unimaginable just a few short years ago. Additionally, powerful computer conferencing programs now provide communication capacities that are designed to simulate the most prominent features of face-to-face classrooms, at a distance and over time.

Our focus in this book is on creative and interactive learning that involves significant and continuous participation and interaction among learners and teachers. We primarily address learning that occurs among groups of learners rather than the independent learner studying alone.

Many educational organizations are experimenting with how they might use these new tools and technologies to extend educational access to previously unserved or underserved audiences; improve the quality of teaching in face-to-face classrooms; and change the nature of the teaching-learning interaction to involve learners more directly in creating effective learning environments. Even with this developing experience base, though, our knowledge is limited when it comes to how we can best organize these new instructional environments. We are constantly learning as we go. This book is an effort to offer you, the actively experimenting teacher, a set of principles and suggestions for further expanding the capabilities and understanding of the online learning environment. We've synthesized these principles and suggestions from a growing literature, from our own online teaching and research activities, and from feedback and suggestions from online learners we've interviewed and queried.

Our goal in this book is to advance the effective practice of teaching and learning online. With that in mind, we hope you'll test our suggestions and give us feedback about both your own experiences in online learning and your use of this book.

The Web-Based Environment

Many educators recognize the potential of the web for transforming their own teaching methods and reaching more learners. In this book, we concentrate on the web as the forum for bringing people together for **formal** education; however, you can apply many of our suggestions to group learning in **informal** web-based settings as well.

You can also implement our suggestions across many **levels** of education, from the K-12 system to higher education to workplace learning. The World Wide Web is ever changing, but as you begin to work online you'll learn to adapt new features and functions of the technology into your courses. For example, the web has created a unique forum for learning that provides increasing opportunities for you and your learners to access video information or listen to radio stations worldwide; join in discussion forums on a multitude of topics; and access millions of content pages on almost any topic imaginable.

Synchronous and Asynchronous Learning

Web-based interactions can be *synchronous* or *asynchronous*. *Synchronous* interactions are those in which learners are online at the same time. Examples of activities that use synchronous communication features include brainstorming, role playing, and discussing course content in real time. *Asynchronous* interactions are those that do not take place in real time. Learners participate in asynchronous course activities at times that are convenient to them. The delayed interaction allows learners to pace themselves and to reflect before contributing to the online discussion.

The Addition of Technology to the Teacher, Learner, and Content of the Classroom

In many instructional contexts, technology beyond the chalkboard and the written word does not play a prominent role in the interchanges among the learner, the teacher, and the content to be learned. However, in online learning, the technology is always present and dominating in terms of the attention it demands from both teacher and learner. As such, it must be addressed continuously and incorporated creatively by both the learner and the teacher, as outlined in the diagram below:

TECHNOLOGY-ASSISTED TEACHING AND LEARNING

Face-to-Face Classroom

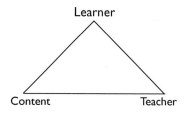

Online Classroom

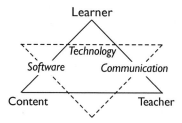

Technology enables learning to occur across distances. However, even when used effectively it is a constant presence in the classroom that must be incorporated conceptually into the instructional and learning plans for the class. When used ineffectively, it can serve as a powerful deterrent for learning.

The Context of This Book

In this book, we refer to online learning as an entirely Internet-based activity. The courses need not have any face-to-face component, yet we are aware that many courses may involve both online interactions and classroom meetings.

We propose that the environment of online learning actively engages both the learner and the teacher with multiple interactive strategies. Our ultimate focus is on the learner. However, we recognize the critical nature of the decisions you must make as a teacher in organizing an effective learning environment. Depending upon the specific context and instructional goals, classrooms may appropriately focus on content, teaching, or technology, as well as on learning.

Our theoretical framework for this book reflects our belief in the efficacy of a learner-centered, constructivist approach, as described in Chapter 1. (Note: Our theoretical foundation for learning is derived from *constructivist learning theory,* which states that effective learning occurs when learners actively construct knowledge through intellectual engagement and personal investment in meaningful and authentic tasks [Brooks and Brooks 1993; Brooks, Brooks, and Association for Supervision and Curriculum Development 1997; Duffy and Jonassen 1991; Fosnot 1996; Lambert et al. 1995; Lebow 1993]. Learners form meaning by actively integrating their previous experiences with new understandings and concepts. For instance, when learners attend class, they come with innate goals and curiosities. Because learning is discovery and transformation of complex information, learners find multiple ways to link the new information with their previous experiences [Conceição-Runlee and Daley 1998].)

Are you ready? Then let's get started.

Chapter 1

BEFORE YOU BEGIN

Before you begin to organize an online course, consider and clarify your own philosophy and assumptions about teaching and learning. Consider also the organizational framework from which you will develop and offer your course; the people you'll work with to develop the course; and the nature of the online environment that you want to create.

This chapter offers you tips on things you need to think about before you decide to offer your course online.

1. Know yourself.

As a teacher, you must know yourself, your assumptions, your learning and teaching preferences, and your strengths and weaknesses. By understanding your own perspectives and abilities, you'll be able to better assist and contribute to the learning of others.

Many tools can help you understand yourself and your own learning and change preferences. Among those tools: the Myers-Briggs Type Indicator (a personality assessment), the David Kolb Learning Style Inventory (1984), the Change Style Indicator (http://www.discoverylearning.net), the Keirsey Temperament Sorter (http://keirsey.com) and, of course, the Kingdomality Medieval Vocational Personality Indicator® (http://www.kingdomality.com), which we described briefly in the Preface of this book. With these guides, your own self-reflection, and your continuing experience in the classroom and online, you'll discover important information about your own teaching style and preferences.

2. Determine your philosophy of teaching and learning.

As you debate whether or not to incorporate online instruction into your course, be sure to consider your own philosophy of teaching and learning. Your philosophical approach to interactive online courses is different from the one you have for content-focused courses on the web.

When you start to think about taking a course online, you must first examine your assumptions about yourself as a teacher and as a learner. Let's take a look at four different philosophical approaches you can explore. We provide some scenarios for which each approach is most useful, and some examples of each approach's application, recognizing that almost all online learning environments will include features from each model.

Teacher-centered. In a teacher-centered course, you organize the course, the content, and the learning activities without a great deal of input from or negotiation with the learners. A teacher-centered approach may be useful when there is a specific amount of content you must convey to the learners. In an online environment, this is often achieved through content-heavy web pages and specific assessment tools like quizzes and homework. Discussion with and among the learners may or may not play a large role in this format. As the teacher, you often direct the learning with resources and lecture-style engagement, but you may not interact or engage with the learners as a group member.

Learner-centered. In a learner-centered course, you structure the course to enable learners to share in the process of selecting and developing content. As is the case in the teacher-centered environment, a continuum exists here as to the level of focus on the learner. On one extreme, you are a fully-participating member of the group who has no unalterable assumptions about the content or direction of the course. In this case, you negotiate with the learners both the content to be covered and the learning strategies to be used. On the other extreme, you may be very structured in the course while offering a limited amount of space in which the learners can make decisions and work with you.

In interactive online courses as we envision them, you the teacher provide a framework for the course, but you offer flexibility and room for negotiation of the content and format. Since an online course requires more preparation than a face-to-face course, it's useful to have such a framework for the course already developed. You can then facilitate the course through discussion and problem-posing dialogue, referring to external resources as needed.

In short, you balance your role as a member of the group, learning with the students, with your role (when necessary) as facilitator and expert. (See Tip 24, "Define Your Role in the Online Classroom" for more teacher roles.)

Learning community-centered. Learning community-centered courses are intentionally created environments that recognize and emphasize the social aspects of learning. Although learning is often pursued for individual reasons, this environment promotes social interaction as a process that is critical for learning. Through the intentional creation of a safe psychological climate, learners with diverse backgrounds are able to learn from each other intensively and cooperatively.

Learning community-centered courses can help you integrate students' experiences with newly presented content, link practice to theory, build students' social and team skills, reduce student boredom and attrition rates, and validate the worth of each participant as a person and learner (Hanna 2000).

Technology-driven. In a technology-driven course, the technology you select dictates many of the decisions you make about the way you establish the course environment and the approach you take to deliver course content. In many cases, you select the technology because it's what's available, or because it's the newest and "best" among other products. Frequently, learner needs and/or your goals as an instructor become secondary to what the technology will allow. In short, the danger of this approach is that technology may force the content and interaction into some predetermined parameters, thus stifling creativity or spontaneity of the course and its members.

Some courses may be fully automated and uploaded so that your role is to design instruction rather than interact directly with the learners. Although this type of course has several benefits and can serve large numbers of learners at a relatively low cost, it resembles an automated training program — and it is not what we refer to as an "interactive online course" in this book.

3. Be a team player.

As an instructor, you may want to work with colleagues to form an instructional design team for your course.

The concept of a team whose members have complementary skills is very important in planning, designing, and implementing online courses. Start the team-building process by defining roles and responsibilities of the team members and communicating those roles and responsibilities to everyone involved. Clearly defined roles and responsibilities provide a foundation for a solid working relationship throughout the course design and development process.

Whether you're using synchronous or asynchronous learning technologies, team members may include:

- an instructor
- a coordinator
- a learner liaison
- an instructional designer
- a graphic designer
- technology personnel
- resource personnel
- administrative personnel.

Depending on the course, the organization, the projected enrollments, and the budget, the design team will grow or shrink in size. In most cases, the instructor (and, often, a technology expert) will perform all of these tasks, especially in primary and secondary classrooms or in situations where developing a single course is not part of a coordinated curriculum, degree sequence, or comprehensive organizational effort.

Instructor. The instructor usually assumes the role of "instructional or content expert." He or she is responsible for planning, implementing, and evaluating instructional activities that are used to teach the course and influence the learning that occurs within it. As the design team grows, the instructor shares responsibility for design and implementation of the course with the other team members.

Coordinator. If the course is part of a larger curriculum, degree program, or course sequence, a coordinator may be involved to organize the program and serve as a liaison between the instructor and other members of the team. The coordinator may also function in other capacities as a part of the team to ensure consistency in course quality, style, promotion, and implementation.

Learner liaison. Many online programs, especially those targeted toward adults, support a position whose responsibilities include being a continuous point of contact for the learners. This "learner liaison" position involves helping learners navigate the organization, solve problems related to organizational structure and policies, and deal with other logistics that might impede the learning process.

Instructional designer. In some cases, an instructional designer is involved to guide the instructor in overall course design and the use of appropriate technologies. This usually occurs when the course is part of a degree program or course sequence meeting certain criteria. Additionally, if the instructor has been hired as an adjunct to teach a course that has already been developed, the instructional designer may have been actively involved with the original course development.

Graphic designer. If the course will use highly specialized graphics or effects, a graphic designer may be involved in creating them. He or she assists in designing specialized computer graphics, visuals and print materials, web-based materials, and whatever else the instructor or instructional designer requests.

Technology personnel. Individuals responsible for equipment setup, network connections, testing, and troubleshooting form the technology personnel. These people must also be knowledgeable about where learners are directed when they have technical problems with software or equipment. Technology personnel often support both teachers and learners with their knowledge of hardware and software applications. Very often, organizations will employ knowledgeable technology personnel in a 24-hours-a-day, seven-days-per-week help desk position. This position can be of great assistance to both teachers and learners, and it is critical as the number of learners in the course increases.

Resource personnel. Resource personnel are responsible for developing or finding readings and other course materials. Resource personnel may include librarians, research assistants (in a university setting), or specialists in the field. Some resource personnel may be invited to be guest speakers, to serve as mentors to the learners, or to act as experts in the field. The particular resource personnel selected for a particular course depends greatly on the topic of the course, its format, and the focus of its material.

Administrative personnel. Administrative personnel are responsible for ensuring an adequate budget for the course, implementing targeted marketing efforts for the course, and overseeing the registration process for the course. Administrative roles vary widely, depending on the organization, but they're always included whenever an online course is offered.

4. Learn new skills for teaching online.

To successfully plan and implement an online course, you need to have a number of specific skills. Understanding the characteristics of the technology is your first responsibility. Other tasks to consider include:

- communicating with your team members
- preparing and following a timeline
- working with design personnel to develop course format and strategies
- scheduling guest experts
- obtaining copyright approvals
- developing contingency plans
- taking care of program logistics
- preparing course resources ahead of time
- providing feedback to learners

5. Understand your audience.

In marketing a program or course, it's important to understand the needs, backgrounds, characteristics, and expectations of the target learners. Online courses that attract participants from diverse locations may have learners with different needs. Some learners, for instance, may require special accommodations, such as large print on course materials, or software programs that assist in decoding graphics or text in a web-based environment.

One way to address the anticipated cognitive or performance needs of your learners is to send them pretests or surveys before the start of the class, or to have them complete portfolio reviews during the course. By understanding the learners' needs, you can vary the presentation of materials to fit diverse learning styles, develop supporting materials, and present content in ways that offer learners different labels for the comprehension of concepts.

6. Understand the online environment.

Multiple components — technology and resources — become essential when you're designing an online teaching environment. Developing an online environment using technology isn't easy when you're unfamiliar with the use of the media and with the resources available to your learners. Your challenge, then, lies in learning how to use the technology while providing technical training, resources, and course content delivery to your learners.

7. Learn about the technology.

Become familiar with your hardware and software and their underlying features and subtleties. While technology that works well may not motivate learners, technology that doesn't work well can cause the learner to give up. So be very concerned with the operation of your hardware and software. Use technology to mediate communication, provide access to your learners, organize your instructional information, and deliver the instruction itself.

8. Learn about your resources.

Become familiar with the learning and technology resources available within your organization. Many organizations, for example, place reserve materials online and offer access to library resources via the web. These resources may be essential in helping your learners access class materials and search for information.

Check with your organization to see which of its library resources are available online. Remember too that most organizations maintain a 24-hours-a-day, seven-days-a-week technology help line. If your organization has no such service, be wary of accepting an online teaching assignment.

9. Recognize the absence of physical presence.

We communicate in a physical environment through a combination of spoken words, writing, and verbal and visual cues that convey both meaning and intent. We're also able to adjust our communication content and intent "on the fly" as we speak, when we perceive that others are misunderstanding us, or when we infer from the reactions of others that our meanings and intent aren't clear.

In a completely online environment, this immediate, informal visual and verbal feedback isn't available to us in a way we're accustomed to both sending and receiving. To some extent, though, you can compensate for this absence of traditionally and culturally communicated body language and other physical cues. As more people join a virtual environment, a new language of cues is being developed, with :) and other symbols being used to express emotive content. For more information about the "netiquette" (Internet etiquette) that has emerged and is emerging, refer to the following web sites:

- http://www.primenet.com/~vez/neti.html
- http://www.albion.com/netiquette/corerules.html
- http://www.xmission.com/~emailbox/netiquette.htm

As a teacher, you may want to prompt your learners to use these textual cues when they're interacting with you and each other. Be aware that, in an online environment, sensitive topics can much more easily elevate to serious situations that become personal. For example, without clearly communicated intentions, humor is difficult to discern and interpret online. Additionally, an individual's interpretation of a message isn't immediately given as feedback as it usually is in spoken conversation.

You and your learners are responsible for creating a space that is safe for all participants. You should share examples of the differences in communication styles and protocols in an online environment. While everyone plays a role in creating and maintaining a safe learning space online, you are that space's guardian.

10. Create multiple spaces for work, interaction, and socializing.

Learning occurs in more than one setting in face-to-face classrooms (for example, as part of before-class conversation, teacher-focused interaction, group work, and after-class relaxation and socialization). You can incorporate similar forums into your online course.

For example, you might organize small groups into one space to respond to content questions or to work on group projects. Or, you could encourage individual learners to post their papers and individual assignments to their own content-oriented web pages. Large-group forums or bulletin boards can answer questions about the technology or offer a space for process reflections. And independent, more informal chat groups or "cyber café" forums can provide a space for social interaction and mingling.

It's important to plan for these spaces and interactions when you're designing your online course.

11. Include multiple types of interactions.

Interaction online can take multiple shapes. One common form of interaction is for a teacher or web page designer to put content onto a web page and for the learners to read it, review it, or be quizzed about it later on — with no actual communication taking place between teacher and learners. Another activity features synchronous chat, during which many people type and communicate with each other at the same time.

Features such as bulletin boards enable discussions to occur asynchronously (over a period of time) as people log in to the conference or online classroom and respond to each other's comments and questions. At times, individual learners may also work together on a document or use the online environment to share materials.

The World Wide Web and its links offer a great resource for data gathering and critique. But in most cases, this individual work should not be the center of your course.

12. Consider which interactions to include.

When you're designing an online course, think in terms of the types of interaction you want to include: learner-to-teacher, learner-to-learner, learner-to-guest expert/community member, learner-to-tools, learner-to-content, or learner-to-environment. Try to include a variety of activities with all kinds of interactions throughout the course.

The table on the next page (adapted from Reigeluth and Moore 1999) illustrates in detail the types of possible interactions.

13. Consider learner-to-teacher interaction.

In the formal sense, learner-to-teacher interaction may include online journals, paper assignments, or quizzes in which learners interact directly with you and receive feedback. In another sense, you and the learners may interact as colleagues within a discussion group — although the influence of your having the power of grading never fully disappears.

14. Consider learner-to-learner interaction.

Learner-to-learner interaction involves learners participating in activities with each other. These activities may include online discussions focusing on problem-based scenarios, problem solving, or case studies; team projects that involve the development of a program; online group discussion based on role assignments; or Internet "scavenger hunts" and resource sharing.

15. Consider learner-to-expert interaction.

Even in a course offered completely online, learners are not confined to the computer for all of their interactions or resources. To enhance the course, learners may invite a community member or guest expert to participate in or contribute to the course. Activities may include interviewing a community member, holding an online discussion with a guest expert, or exploring issues with practitioners. After drawing on outside individuals and resources, the learners can bring their experiences and knowledge back and share it with the rest of the class.

TYPES OF INTERACTIONS

Human Interactions	Types of Activities
Learner-Teacher	• Self-regulated learning. (A web-based conferencing environment may require participants to manage their time, process information, plan and manage their resources, and evaluate their own work. Learners can seek help when they need it.) • Collaborative problem solving. (As the teacher, you post a problem to be solved by individual learners.) • You and the learners participate in the collective activities and knowledge sharing. • You observe, monitor, and provide feedback to the learners. • You facilitate group processes by responding to questionable situations, such as discussion problems, group dynamics issues, or misunderstandings.
Learner-Learner	• Learners complete group work to improve their social and critical thinking skills. • Learners access group knowledge and support through collaborative problem solving. • Learners design a website for an instructional program.
Learner-Guest Expert or Learner-Community Member	• Learners collaborate with guests on projects to gain diverse expertise. • Learners discuss real-life situations with practitioners in the community. • Learners work together with community members to solve problems and share knowledge.

Non-Human Interactions	Types of Activities
Learner-Tools	• Learners operate software (text copying and pasting, file transferring, image grabbing, brainstorming, outlining, and flow charting). • Learners manipulate software (changing contents, values, and/or parameters to verify, test, and extend understanding). • Learners communicate using the software (promoting discourse, sharing ideas, reviewing work, asking questions, and collaborating).
Learner-Content	• Learners work with and make sense of the information available on the web, in books, and in databases.
Learner-Environment	• Learners work with resources and simulations (web-based searches, image libraries, source documents, and online databases).

16. Consider learner-to-content interaction.

In learner-to-content interaction, you the teacher play an indirect role by posting content or directing the learners to work on their own. The learners' activities may include searching for, managing, and making sense of information. For example, learners might interact with content through reading text, viewing web sites, or searching databases.

17. Consider learner-to-technology interaction.

For learner-to-technology interaction, some activities may involve learners in completing tasks using a software program. With such a variety of software available, you can adapt various applications and incorporate them into your online course. Examples might include simulations; software operation and manipulation; copying and pasting (e.g., from a word processing document to a web conferencing program); file transferring (e.g., web page design); image grabbing (e.g., uploading an image from the Internet and using it as an observation assignment); brainstorming; outlining; flowcharting; and accessing "ask the expert" sites.

Beware, though: It may be easy to overuse these methods of interaction and detract from the human interaction of the course.

18. Establish the preferred class size.

Decide the size of your class before you design the course. While successful courses have been developed with sizes in multiples of one hundred, it's important to recognize that escalating size increases the logistical support you'll need and reduces the direct interaction you'll have with your learners.

For most classes that are taught primarily asynchronously and in groups where interaction is a key feature of the course, we suggest an upper limit of twenty to thirty learners per instructor. If you decide that learner interaction isn't important to meeting your course objectives, you can increase class size. However, know that with increasing class size comes greater emphasis on content delivery vs. learner mastery.

For online courses or discussion groups meeting synchronously, we recommend an upper limit of five learners per discussion group. Larger groups reduce both the opportunity to participate and the overall quality of the discussion.

19. Consider team-based learning.

Team-based learning is an excellent strategy to use because online learning presents rich opportunities for creating teams for problem solving, project development, and discussion.

However, team-based learning requires a number of elements to be truly effective. Most importantly, you must be knowledgeable and aware of the characteristics and preferences of your other team members, and you must develop trust among them.

Before selecting team-based learning as an instructional strategy, consider how team-based learning might contribute to your instructional goals, how the time frame for the course supports the development of teams, and how you can support team communication. Team-based learning requires rich communication above all. If you decide to use a team-based learning approach, you should provide a context that supports the development of both knowledge and trust.

For more information on team-based learning, see Hanna and Conceição-Runlee (1999).

20. Form personal relationships online.

As in any course, the first class meeting and the introductions among participants set the tone for what is to come. So you can and should establish strong connections, both personal and course related, in the online environment.

Participants learn from and about each other through not only **what** they say, but also **how** they say it. Relationships can form within the group as well as through the sidebar communication that occurs one-on-one via e-mail or personal mailboxes. The online communication among participants contributes greatly to the eventual outcomes of the course.

21. Develop learning communities.

A learning community is a group of people who have come together to form a culture of learning in which everyone is involved in a collective effort of understanding. Learning communities are commonly formed in an interactive online environment when a group of learners forms to expand its collective knowledge and skills, thus supporting the growth of individual knowledge and skills.

The communities that develop may be formal or informal, as in the example of young people using web browser features like "instant Messenger" to keep in touch with each other. (Note: "instant Messaging" is a convention supported by several web browsers, including Netscape, Microsoft Internet Explorer, and the America Online browser. It enables real-time, synchronous, text-based conversation and dialogue among multiple users, similar to an online chat.)

When you're using the learning community concept in your online course, be sure to encourage learners to share their expertise. Be sure as well to emphasize learning how to learn, and to create mechanisms to help participants share what they've learned with each other. It's important that community participants define their roles as learners and articulate their learning processes, plans, goals, and assumptions.

Examples of activities that support learning communities include class discussion, individual and group research, group projects and presentations, and collaborative problem solving. During the discussion process, knowledge and ideas are formulated and exchanged through discourse, and learners are expected to provide feedback to each other.

22. Learn through dialogue.

Hopefully, your participants will learn through dialogue, respond to ideas, and continue discussions by offering their concise, thoughtful comments. It's essential, however, that neither the learners nor you criticize or judge others' ideas as worthless just because those ideas are "different."

As the teacher, encourage learners to reflect interactively with each other and the course content. Conflict may arise as the learners become more comfortable with each other and the technology. But most conflict is helpful as a learning tool, and most of the time the learners will be able to work through it. If the conversation becomes offensive (flaming) to some members of the group, you can always step in and talk to those involved so that together you can work out a solution.

23. Be prepared and flexible.

The online environment requires a different amount and style of preparation for you as a teacher. In a face-to-face classroom, the walls of the room define the dominant space for discussion. In an online environment, however, you must define the space for discussion before the class begins by outlining what kinds of interactions will be used and through what format.

Online learning requires — of both you and your learners — a different mindset, different discipline, and different time management. As such, you must define whether your course focuses on process or content **before** you develop the course's structure, assignments, and assessment strategies. Online courses that focus on *process* involve the development of specific steps or procedures to expedite learning. Online courses that focus on *content* are aimed at helping learners learn a specific subject matter. Both approaches can use discussion, research, idea or resource sharing, and group projects.

Give your learners structure and guidelines when you're planning and organizing the materials for your online course. You can decide upon most of the structure of the class and the objectives for the learners before the class begins. But you'll still need to be flexible within the course framework so that learners can offer their input and negotiation.

24. Define your role in the online classroom.

When teaching online, you may have more than one role, depending on the instructional strategy you're using. Consider the following points in defining your role as an instructor:

- Set attainable goals for your learners, and use benchmarks to acknowledge their growth.
- State your expectations and minimum participation requirements upfront.

- Negotiate norms with the learners.
- Be accessible but not dominating online.
- Consider carefully your modeling and mentoring processes and ideologies.
- Be a coach and cheerleader.
- Learn with and from the class members.

25. Clarify your expectations of learners' roles.

As a teacher, you have assumptions about what it means to be a learner. In an interactive online course, the learner's role becomes more complex and more active. So before you plan your online course, clarify your expectations of learners' roles and contributions.

Following are some potential expectations you might have for learners regarding the roles they play in the interactive online environment.

26. Expect learners to be present online and to avoid passively observing.

One of the great advantages of online learning, especially in an asynchronous mode, is that there is no competition for "airtime" during the class. Each learner can contribute his or her ideas at a comfortable pace. Some learners are more comfortable communicating verbally; others communicate more easily in writing. You, as the teacher, should discuss these preferences at the beginning of the course and indicate your initial expectations for participation, which may include logging in to the class, reading what others have said during discussion, and responding to those ideas. After a week or two, you might revisit your expectations during class briefly, and ask for agreement with or modification of your initial expectations.

27. Expect learners to create, share, and hold knowledge and experiences.

In a completely online environment, participants experience a unique process of learning. You can use this new experience as a tool for teaching.

Each participant comes to the online education experience with prior knowledge about teaching and learning (since each has gone through prior schooling). Each person also brings to the classroom a wide range of other knowledge. It's important that you and your learners have opportunities to recognize and value the knowledge that all participants hold, and try to connect new learning to previous experiences and understandings. For example, learners who are more familiar with the technology can help the first-timers with their questions or problems. Or, people with direct experience in the subject being taught can share their stories with their classmates.

Engaging in discussion about not only the **content** of the course, but also the **process** of the course helps to support these linkages among people, so that they can share their knowledge while learning the new information.

28. Expect learners to be self-motivated and self-directed.

Online learning emphasizes learner responsibility — even in courses that are largely teacher centered. Thus, learners must be able to set a schedule and stick to it; organize their time effectively to incorporate their readings and online discussions into their normal schedules; and complete assignments within the suggested timeframes set for the course.

As the teacher, you can make the learners aware of these expectations in a number of ways. For example, you could:

- Give your learners a brief quiz to assess their readiness for online learning.
- Discuss your requirements at the beginning of class.
- Ask the students to create and share with you calendars or learning contracts showing when they will schedule course activities.

These assignments and activities will help your students consider the important self-motivation and self-direction elements of online learning.

29. Expect learners to manage their time effectively.

In an online environment, time management can be an obstacle for many learners. Online courses move quickly and require self-discipline. Interactions are omnipresent but never immediate. The online discussion is always "there," just a click away, but response time is random.

Both you and your learners will soon realize that you have to participate in the class at least every other day in order to stay connected. At times, the online environment may be overwhelming in terms of the number of comments to keep up with and the fact that the whole process is ongoing. That's why you and your learners will benefit from developing a personal schedule of deadlines at the beginning of the course and sticking to it. By helping and expecting learners to manage their time, you'll keep them on track.

30. Expect learners to be ready to learn.

Online courses may be viewed as "easier" to teach because you, as the teacher, can work from home on your own time or while you're away from your workplace. Yet, as the learners participating in an interactive online course quickly come to realize, the class is with you and with them all the time — and they are required to participate and respond more than they would in a face-to-face class.

When coming into an interactive online course, the participants need to be ready to learn, and to persist through unfamiliar technology as well as the subject matter itself. Learning looks different in an interactive online class; participants may need to be more self-directed and attentive. However, information stays with the participants longer because they reflect upon it through discussion instead of just reading it and setting it aside for the exam.

31. Expect learners to troubleshoot problems.

Problems often occur unexpectedly in an online class. The server with the computer conference goes off-line. A learner's computer crashes. A document is accidentally erased. Learners need to be able to get help easily, but they also need to be able to approach a problem with multiple points of advice and solution.

In addition to communicating with a 24-hours-a-day, seven-days-a-week help desk for technology problems, the students should have a "buddy" in the class to whom they can turn. They should also be able to reach you in multiple ways, including voice mail, e-mail, and fax. Keep in mind that learners go to class in an online environment seven days a week. So having some plan for difficult problems — a plan that students can take advantage of even on the weekends — is important.

32. Expect learners to contribute to the class discussions.

To ensure contribution from your students, you may want to require a minimum number of postings from each learner each week.

Contributions can vary in style and quality, of course. When contributing to class discussions, you and your learners should share ideas in the form of meaningful and concise answers rather than one-word responses. In order to gain the most from the material and the interactions, the participants should also contribute postings that are reflective and thoughtful.

Since each learner plays a role in the discussions, and since you the teacher also engage as a learner, participants should direct their comments not only to you but also to their fellow classmates. This approach opens up the discussion for everyone to be included and for all contributions to be valued. If participants want an answer from a specific person, they can address their comments to that person. If, on the other hand, participants wish to address the whole class, they may simply say, "Hello everyone."

Participants should always be respectful of others' ideas, but they should also feel free to share different perspectives or opinions.

33. Expect learners to teach others and facilitate the experience.

Learners in online courses have enormous opportunities to "be the teacher" whether in troubleshooting the software and the technology or in forming and communicating their ideas about the content of the class. As the teacher, build on this capability by creating formal opportunities for learners to share their learning with each other. Learners are challenged when they know that what they learn matters to others.

34. Expect learners to act as collegial members of the class.

Online learning requires different dynamics due to the lack of physical cues. The written language may be misinterpreted and cause a level of discomfort among the members of an online community. That's why participants in your course should maintain a level of collegiality and respect for others' ideas and experiences.

35. Expect learners to review readings and materials thoughtfully and reflectively.

In an online course, class materials can appear in the form of web-based texts, tutorials, file attachments, simulations, or other resources. At times, the amount of material may be overwhelming, or some material might even be overlooked due to its location. You may post material directly on the web or in a web conferencing environment, send material to learners via e-mail attachment, or put material in an electronic reserve area of your organization's web server. Whatever the case, be sure to stress to your learners that they must review all of the materials thoughtfully and reflectively so that they can keep pace in the course.

36. Expect learners to provide timely, meaningful feedback to you and their fellow learners.

Since the online classroom is always accessible, issues and ideas can move quickly. When learners have a statement to make to you or their classmates, they should write and submit it right away; otherwise, the next time they read the class postings their idea may no longer fit in with the discussion.

To make interactions more meaningful, it's helpful for you and your learners to make connections between and among the various postings. When you do, the learners can then more easily follow the train of thought.

Be sure you also encourage learners to make timely, constructive suggestions on how you can improve the class.

37. Expect learners to be leaders.

All learners in an interactive online class may play multiple leadership roles throughout their time together. Thus, it's important for the learners to embrace the opportunities presented by this format to facilitate group discussion, cooperate on a team project, and mentor others along the way. By acting as leaders, the learners can take ownership of the course and better connect with what's being taught.

38. Expect learners to "listen" to others.

In a face-to-face classroom, learners can tune out the lecture or discussion as they wish. But in an online environment, the learners must actively read each other's postings and "listen" to what's being said. By having all interaction take the shape of written words, the learners can go back and reread comments to ascertain the intent and the actual meaning behind the words. The learners do not just hear noise and useless words. Rather, they can and should concentrate on, focus on, and process the ideas being shared.

39. Expect learners to communicate by addressing each other, not just you.

The interactive online course is a collaboration between and among you and your learners. As such, each participant constructs his or her own knowledge and shares that knowledge with others in the group. To help your learners build personal and collegial relationships with each other, encourage them to share their comments and ideas with everyone, not just you. By approaching participation in this manner, you'll encourage everyone to feel welcome to respond to a point or an idea. You'll also relieve yourself from being unilaterally responsible for keeping the discussion going — an impossible challenge in the online environment.

40. Expect learners to be proactive.

Technology doesn't always work, and sometimes a learner might be having trouble without your realizing it. At times like these, learners need to be proactive and inform you.

Learners must also ask questions immediately if they don't understand what to do with the technology or in a course assignment.

41. Expect learners to observe the process.

Learning happens on many levels in online classrooms. In an interactive course, learners should avoid focusing solely on the assignments and the products of the course; they should also observe the process of the online discussions. Keeping abreast of the continuous flow of online discussions helps the participants stay connected with the course and each other.

42. Establish a contingency plan.

Whenever you're working with technology, you can never guarantee that it will do what you want it to do. So when you're constructing your course, be sure to develop a contingency plan and share it with the learners before the course begins.

Most organizations have a help line that offers learners technical support over the phone. Include this number in your course syllabus. Also, pair your learners into groups of "technology buddies" that include one learner who has more experience with computers and another learner who may need more help.

Have an alternative way for your learners to reach you (such as a different e-mail address, phone number, or fax number) in case of emergency. And, as the teacher, test the technology often, back up your files, and make friends with the technical support personnel within your organization.

Chapter 2

MYTHS AND CONSTRAINTS OF ONLINE TEACHING AND LEARNING

Online teaching and learning is a growing field with many misconceptions. In this chapter, we critique the most common myths and discuss some of the current constraints for learning in the online environment.

We recognize that this is just a sampling of the myths of and constraints for teaching online, and that commonly recognized myths and constraints also change over time. Still, we've attempted to offer myths and constraints that are current, and that will likely have substantial staying power.

MYTHS OF ONLINE TEACHING AND LEARNING

43. Myth: Learners are unable to adapt to the online environment.

As the research on learning styles shows (Gardner 1993; Kolb 1977 and 1984; Sanchez and Gunawardena 1998), people learn in multiple ways and through multiple senses. Although the preference for one learning style may be stronger, most people can learn in a variety of ways.

In the online environment, learners acquire much of the course content through reading and writing. But you could encourage some of the learners to read discussion comments aloud to have some audio stimulation. Or, you could add to the course links or references to audio or video files so that the learners would have the opportunity to stimulate multiple senses.

44. Myth: The instructor has to know how to do everything.

Teaching in an online environment should be a team effort. You should be able to call upon technology specialists, instructional designers, and many others to help you develop and implement your course. Often, because there is a team of people working together, you'll be compelled to reflect upon your own assumptions and preferences — thus, the course improves.

45. Myth: Time requirements for teachers are lower in an online environment.

Often, online teaching is viewed as a quick way to get content to learners. Many teachers see it, at first, as a potential time saver. Unfortunately, though, this is not the case. As we mentioned earlier in this book, online, interactive courses are open twenty-four hours a day, seven days a week. The tasks of establishing a course framework and rethinking your curriculum to adapt it to the online environment (with or without a design team) are time consuming and challenging.

46. Myth: Online classrooms aren't conducive to group interaction and activities.

The opportunity for group interaction in the online learning setting depends upon the software you're using and the educational model you've selected. In the model we're discussing here, group interaction is central to the learning that takes place. Conferencing software offers many opportunities for interaction in multiple group settings that you determine and negotiate with your learners.

These organized spaces can include settings for small-group work; reflections on process; socialization and informal, "outside of class" interactions; and a "help desk" for technical challenges.

47. Myth: Online classrooms aren't as social as face-to-face classrooms.

Parker Palmer (1998) reminds us that classrooms are simply spaces that have been organized especially to promote learning among a community of people whose learning goals are similar. The degree and nature of interaction among participants in face-to-face classrooms vary greatly, and the same is true in online classrooms. Online courses can be very lonely, or they can be very social and interactive in nature.

You, as the instructor, are responsible for creating the types of spaces learners want and need, and for sensing your learners' expectations. You must also gauge how important social interaction is to the participants. You can use a variety of techniques, described in this book, to facilitate greater interaction and community among your learners.

One interesting phenomenon that you should keep in mind: Many online learners say they end up knowing their online co-learners more deeply than they would in a class where they would all be physically present with each other.

48. Myth: The number of learners in online classrooms can be unlimited.

Many people believe that one of the benefits of online education is that a single instructor can work with many more learners than he or she might in a face-to-face classroom without affecting the quality of the learning experience, diminishing the content to be learned, or affecting the degree of learner satisfaction. However, socially constructed online learning demands a lot of time (online) from you, even when you organize it effectively to take full advantage of learners' involvement in their own education.

Unless you're contemplating what might be known as simply a "content dump" of materials onto the web (which is not what this book is about), you'll need to carefully develop a plan for providing interaction among you and your learners. Demand for interaction defines the size of face-to-face classrooms and the nature of the interactions within those classrooms; the demand for interaction has a similar effect upon online classrooms.

49. Myth: Technology will always work.

Of course, technology (including software) doesn't always work. And technology that doesn't work — or that is so complex that it limits you and your learners as you attempt to achieve the learning goals for the class — can be a powerful demotivator for learning.

Yet even when technology works well and effectively, the time, resources, planning, and organizational skill required to achieve this feat go largely unrecognized. Many instructors view their role as being unrelated to the operation and support of technology, but they're on the "front lines" when problems arise. That's why you must keep in mind several related ideas and suggestions:

- Plan your use of technology carefully.
- Understand the technology as fully as possible.
- Provide 24-hours-a-day, seven-days-a-week learner assistance whenever possible.
- Give learners detailed instructions on what they should do when the technology doesn't work.
- Develop a backup emergency plan when all else fails, as sometimes will occur.

50. Myth: The course will market itself; post it on the web and they will come.

The web is a big place, and it is growing astronomically each month. As a result, many schools, colleges, universities, and corporations are now developing online courses.

Unless your course has a predefined audience that is delineated and organized well in advance, marketing your course online can be a significant challenge for both you and your organization. So find out when you'll know who's going to be enrolled in your class. Get names and contact information as soon as you can. Will the learners have had experience with the technology and the software you're using? Can you contact the learners well before the beginning of the class? If so, you can inform them early on about specific course elements, including preferred or required technology and software, readings, proxies, and other matters for which preparation on the learner's part will maximize opportunities for developing an effective online learning environment.

51. Myth: Learners will always understand your intended expectations for them from your clearly written syllabus.

In an online course, the class syllabus appears in a text-based format, and discussion about its content is difficult. Thus, learners don't always immediately understand the details of class materials. In addition, learners may accidentally overlook materials because those materials are located online.

So be sure to provide on the syllabus a detailed explanation of your intended expectations of learners. Organize the syllabus in a friendly and conversational way so that your learners will move through the course requirements efficiently. Use the syllabus as a working document to check each learner's progress and his or her understanding of your expectations.

CONSTRAINTS FOR INTERACTIVE ONLINE TEACHING AND LEARNING

Not everyone is comfortable with learning online. Here are some additional potential constraints that apply to an online course situation more so than they would to a face-to-face classroom setting.

52. Constraint: Fear of technology.

Some people embrace new technologies eagerly, while others are afraid of change and the pressures technology has on their understanding of the world. Although technology is all around us, some people are afraid to use it. Especially for many adults, computers are new and foreign. Thus, they add to the level of anxiety that might interfere with a particular learner's overall education and satisfaction.

Most of the people in this "category" won't consider taking a course online and will struggle greatly if they're required to enroll.

Yet, in many cases, these are the people who wind up learning the most in and from the course.

53. Constraint: Different levels of technology skills.

Learners enter the online classroom with widely differing levels of expertise in technology. This is almost inevitable in a class of any size, and it can present you with both challenges and opportunities.

The challenges may include adapting the pace of the course to allow time for those learners who need to upgrade their skills. The opportunities may include the possibility of teaming technically proficient learners with those who are less proficient so that they can be "technology buddies."

54. Constraint: Literacy levels.

Since most of the interaction in an online course is written, a learner may be at a disadvantage if he or she has a low literacy level. Some online courses are directed at improving literacy skills, but most courses require participants to express themselves and understand others through the written word.

55. Constraint: Ability to type and use the keyboard.

Again, since most interaction in an online course is typed, learners should be able to type at a reasonable level. This is not as important if the course is offered asynchronously; however, if the course meets synchronously, the ability to type (or not type) well can determine who says the most. (Note: With the advent of speech recognition software, this is becoming less of a problem. But it is still something you should carefully consider.)

56. Constraint: Access to a computer and an Internet connection.

In a completely online environment, the computer acts as the mediator for all interactions. However, the computers and the soft-

28

ware being used are only tools that enable learning and interaction among you and your learners.

Remember that each learner must have access to working tools (a computer, software, and an Internet connection) in order to participate fully. Research shows a "digital divide" and a dramatic disparity of access among urban, suburban, and rural populations, and among socio-economic groups and racial and ethnic communities (National Telecommunications and Information Administration 1998).

57. Constraint: The comfort of physical work space.

The physical environment where each of your learners works can determine the quality of the online teaching and learning experience. So encourage students to have comfortable chairs that support their weight, because they'll often be required to sit for long periods of time as they correspond with their fellow learners and complete projects.

Be sure, too, that learners get clear, non-flickering computer screens (to prevent eye irritation or headaches).

Finally, encourage learners to work in rooms that are conducive to learning and that don't have too many distractions.

The advice above goes for you too! If you're uncomfortable in your work space, your ability to teach will be impaired.

58. Constraint: Having a disability.

Consider in advance how you'll address issues of access to your classroom environment and the materials you use. Many physical disabilities, such as those involving sight, hearing, and movement, can be effectively addressed in online environments through the application of specialized technologies developed for those specific purposes.

Beyond planning for learners with special needs, you should also create a process for identifying the resources you can employ in specific instances. You might initiate a discussion of this topic with the appropriate individual in your organization — for example, your program administrator, your technology support person, or the lead instructional designer of your development team. Many excellent resources are available online; we offer you a few of them in Appendix B of this book.

59. Constraint: Not being able to correspond in the language of the course.

It's critical to be able to communicate in the language of the course being offered in order to benefit from the interaction. With the worldwide nature of the Internet, more and more learners are crossing virtual borders and enrolling for courses. Thus, assessing your prospective learners' language proficiencies is another good reason to communicate with your learners before your course begins.

60. Constraint: Reaching across multiple time zones.

Because online education permits asynchronous learning, it can be particularly effective in connecting learners across multiple time zones. At the same time, your efforts to build into your course real-time, synchronous interactions, or to incorporate systematic, team-based activities, may be hampered by the different work, leisure, and sleep schedules of learners spread across many time zones. So be sure to keep this factor in mind as you develop and implement your online course.

Chapter 3

ORGANIZING THE ONLINE COURSE

Once you've decided to offer your course online, there are many details you must address. This chapter provides tips on how to structure the class format, content, syllabus, timeline, use of technology, and evaluation.

61. Identify the course design.

For a typical course, you usually develop the instructional design beforehand by determining specific content, readings, and resources. In an online course, the element of technology also enters the mix. This section discusses the issues you need to think about when you're organizing your course design.

62. Consider course goals and objectives.

In developing a course, you begin by identifying goals and objectives that you wish to achieve with your learners. These can be specific goals of measurable achievement, or they can be more fluid, abstract goals of widening learners' perspectives or helping them see some aspect of life in a new way.

To develop an online course (or any other course), you need to clarify these goals and objectives and write them so that you can clearly communicate them to learners and others working on the course.

63. Consider content.

Once you've specified your goals and objectives, it's time to make some decisions about content. What will you include? What methods will you use to convey the content? In an interactive online course, some content and methods work better than others.

Help learners think about a subject by using case studies related to real-life situations, problems to be solved, and controversial issues to be explored. When you begin having interactions with and among your learners, pose your content as open-ended questions so that the learners can discuss it. And remember: Whenever possible, help learners draw upon their own experiences as they consider the content.

64. Consider readings.

Select readings that provide different perspectives on the course topic. Since the learners already have access to the Internet, use the World Wide Web for some of the readings. However, don't neglect the value and convenience of printed books and journal articles as well.

65. Consider resources.

Become familiar with the resources available within your organization. Many organizations place reserve materials online and provide online access to library resources via the web. These resources may be essential to learners as they attempt to acquire class materials and search for information. Check with your organization for information on learner access to the library and other resources.

66. Consider copyright issues.

Copyright tends to be one of the least familiar areas of concern for most online teachers. But **don't** overlook it — because while giving your learners access to information and using technology for teaching, you may unwittingly enter into a very litigious zone.

Understand copyright law so that you can protect your own work and respect the work of others. Be aware that copyright does not cover the protection of ideas themselves; rather, it protects the **format** of the expression of ideas.

Copyright issues you should understand involve the medium, the factors that determine eligibility for "fair use" and the "10 percent rule." The concern with the medium involves the distribution of copyrighted work in any form. *Fair use* deals with a provision in copyright law allowing for **limited** use of copyrighted material without the owner's permission. Examples of fair use include portions of work that are used for the purposes of criticism, comment, news reporting, teaching scholarship, or research. The *10 percent rule* suggests that using 10 percent or less of a total work is considered fair use. The 10 percent rule usually applies to classroom copying and music.

For more information on copyright and the classroom, refer to Tallman (2000) and Bruwelheide (1997). Additionally, discuss any concerns you have concerning copyright and intellectual property with the appropriate professional in your organization; you'll likely find this person in your library or, perhaps, in your legal department.

67. Determine methods of delivery.

Computer technology and online software change every day, and there are many different applications that can support interactive online teaching and learning.

Online programs (software applications) can be either *interactive* or *non-interactive.* Here we discuss the application types without referring to specific software packages. For a list of current software programs, refer to Appendix A.

68. Consider interactive applications.

Interactive applications are computer programs that enable two or more people to interact while online. Among these applications are chat functions, bulletin boards, discussion groups, shared documents, and e-mail.

Interaction within these applications can be either *synchronous* (real time), like a chat, or *asynchronous,* like a bulletin board a learner can read or add to at his or her convenience. In an interactive online classroom, many of these capabilities can serve different functions. But most often, discussion groups and bulletin boards serve as the primary methods of course interaction.

69. Consider non-interactive applications.

Non-interactive applications are computer programs that don't require human interaction. You can use these programs for quizzes, web postings, streaming audio/video, external links, content pages, and message or comment boards put on a web page. In many online courses, such functions supplement or reinforce the interactive applications. They can also simplify the assessment of learners' knowledge and make course evaluations anonymous.

Non-interactive applications have many positive uses, but we urge you not to be herded into a teaching philosophy or format that is determined solely by the application and tools you're using. Remember your own style, and make sure the tools you use and the way you use them will shape the learning outcomes you want and value.

70. Give learners appropriate advance information.

When possible, before your course begins and once you know who's registered, contact your learners to tell them about your expectations for the course and to gather some preparatory information from them.

71. Tell learners about the computer hardware and software they'll need.

In a letter or phone call to registered learners prior to the start of your course, remind the learners that they'll be participating in an **online** class. Make sure they have the software and hardware they'll need to access and participate in the course. And give them information about the technical support available to them.

72. Tell learners about the level of computing proficiency they'll need.

Interview the registered learners about their familiarity with computers and their level of computing proficiency. This information will help you match up "technology buddies" later on in the course.

73. Tell learners about the level of course content and the course's time expectations.

In your letter or phone call, and also in your syllabus, be sure to include information on the level of course content, your expectations about participation in the course, and a description of the course's projects and activities. This information will act as a screening tool for the course. It will also help you adjust the course to the learners' needs.

74. Decide and communicate what's private and what's public.

Teaching in an interactive online environment depends on establishing a safe, trusting learning community where learners can share their experiences, opinions, and ideas related to the course. Thus, it's important to help students develop personal relationships with their classmates so that all of the learners can speak freely and learn together.

That being said, there is a line you should define about how much information participants can and should share publicly and privately with the group. In a face-to-face classroom, words are spoken and forgotten, and they usually aren't recorded. Additionally, everyone can see who's attending and listening to the conversation. But in an online classroom, all conversation is recorded and saved. And in some cases, there may be other people who are reviewing the interactions and conversations. In other words, although online communications are supposed to be safe from outside eyes, there is a greater chance of disclosure than is the case in the face-to-face classroom. So it's essential for both you and your learners to be aware that information might be shared with others. That way, no one will put himself or herself at undue risk.

75. Develop course details.

Whenever you're developing a course there are many details you must address. This section focuses on some of those details, such as the discussion guidelines, the syllabus, content organization, the course timeline, and course assignments.

76. Establish discussion guidelines.

Establishing guidelines for participant postings is an important aspect of online teaching (and learning). Doing so gives learners a sense of knowledge and a structure for their online discussions.

Your guidelines may cover the length of online responses, file attachment formats, the nature of threaded discussions, and deadlines for postings. (Note: Your guidelines may, to some degree, be contingent upon the conferencing system you're using.)

77. Develop a flexible syllabus.

When developing your syllabus, imagine it as a flexible framework for the course. Use a topic-driven outline that features space for more or less in-depth exploration of the content. In an interactive course, the learners will likely have their own learning agenda. Thus, flexibility also helps them in accomplishing their goals.

(Note: In the syllabus, be sure to add information about your expectations for participation, as well as where the learners can find technical support. In many cases, the syllabus becomes the "learner handbook" for the course.)

78. Organize content into modules or units.

Modules or units provide structure and a sense of content organization for your learners. So be sure to provide small chunks of assignments, to set limits on the length of learners' posts, and to outline specific requirements for those posts. By offering structure and a series of short assignments, you'll keep your learners focused on the course.

When determining the order of your course's content, cover the best content first to keep learners interested. Keep the readings and content logically sequenced by "chunking" information into manageable pieces. When you assign readings, rank the importance of the readings and estimate the amount of time learners will need to set aside for them. One estimate is that most people reading non-fiction will cover twenty pages in an hour. For highly technical information the time slows to ten pages an hour. And for fiction, most learners can read forty pages an hour (Draves 2000).

79. Create a timeline.

Be aware of the dynamics of time management. Depending on the type of course you're designing (content-focused or process-focused), consider providing chronological, developmental, or process-oriented timelines.

For content-focused courses, you might use the chronological approach to distribute course content throughout the course period. For process-focused courses, you might begin the course with a set of competencies that go from simple to complex following a certain developmental process.

Divide the class content into units or modules to help your learners manage the course timeline. Give detailed information about dates of materials being covered and deadlines. Some online instructors even recommend establishing a "no post" or "reading only" day once a week to guard against burnout in web-based course work (Buchanan 2000).

80. Develop assignments.

Learners are ultimately responsible for completing course assignments. However, you have a duty to provide detailed guidelines for this task. At the beginning of your course, be sure to give your learners guidelines, policies, and assignment descriptions.

Course assignments themselves may feature papers, projects, group activities, journal writing, and resource sharing.

81. Decide about evaluation techniques to use.

Evaluation is the process of gathering information about the worth or quality of learning or instruction. Why? So that you can make decisions to increase the worth or quality of the learning or instruction.

Evaluation helps you identify content areas that are unclear or confusing, recognize content areas that need revision, and gather the evidence you need to support those revisions. As you design your course activities and assignments, then, you should continuously consider how you'll evaluate your learners and assess the effectiveness of your course.

82. Evaluate your learners.

You can evaluate your learners before, during, and after your instruction.

Evaluation before instruction — which may include a pretest — helps you identify learners' pre-instructional knowledge and skill levels, focus learners' attention on the main topics to be covered in the course, and determine a point of comparison with learners' pre-instructional knowledge and skill.

Evaluation during the course, also called formative evaluation, helps you identify the knowledge and skills learners have gained in the course to date. It also:

- allows you to determine whether or not to introduce new content

- gives you feedback on the learners' learning processes

- signals whether learners need additional practice or work in certain areas

- refocuses the learners' attention.

Evaluation after the course, also called summative evaluation, measures what learners have learned, finalizes decisions about grades, and reviews new knowledge and skills the learners have gained in taking the course.

83. Assess course effectiveness.

You can assess your course's effectiveness before (pilot test), during (formative evaluation), and after (summative evaluation) a module, unit, or lesson. To evaluate your instructional improvement on a continuous cycle, you might consider answering the following questions (Newby, Stepich, Lehman, and Russell 2000):

Before Instruction

- How well is the instruction likely to work?
- Will the instruction hold learners' interest?
- Is there an alternative way to organize the instruction to make better use of available time and resources?

During Instruction

- What obstacles are learners encountering, and how can they be overcome?
- What can be done to maintain learner motivation?
- How can these learners be helped to better progress through the instruction?

After Instruction

- What improvements could be made in the instruction for future use? What revisions have the highest priority?
- Did learners find the instruction interesting, valuable, and meaningful?
- Were the selected instructional methods, media, and materials effective in helping learners learn?

STRATEGIES FOR EVALUATING LEARNING

There are a variety of techniques you can use to evaluate learners' learning. These strategies can help learners increase their learning through continuous self-renewal and self-evaluation.

Examples of effective learning evaluation techniques include quizzes, essays, portfolios, performance evaluations, interviews, journals, reflective papers, web site development, learner participation figures, peer assessment, and learner self-assessment.

84. Use quizzes.

As you well know, *quizzes* test learners' knowledge by posing questions. In an online environment, you can post quizzes on a web site, attach them to an e-mail, or post them as regular messages.

Your can create quiz questions that are true-false, matching, multiple-choice, completion and short-answer, or essay.

When developing online quizzes, be sure to connect questions to specific learning objectives. Also, make certain you provide clear, explicit directions, and that you use vocabulary appropriate to that of your learners.

85. Use essays.

Essays assess higher-level cognitive skills. Thus, you can use essays to have your learners analyze, reflect, compare, justify, contrast, compile, interpret, or formulate conclusions.

When using essays to measure your learners' competencies, consider including specific directions by phrasing questions or statements clearly (use terms such as "compare," "contrast," "formulate," "discuss," "define," etc.). That way, your learners will understand what you expect.

Additionally, give the students options so that they can write about topics that interest them. Focus on personal perspectives if your goal is to help your learners formulate and express their opinions and attitudes.

Finally, be consistent in grading learner essays. If possible, go through all the answers to a particular question at the same time so that you can evenly compare learners' answers to the criteria you've selected to measure success.

86. Use portfolios.

A *portfolio* is a compilation of work, developed by the learner, that demonstrates what he or she knows and can do. The portfolio documents the learner's efforts, development, or accomplishments throughout the course by showing the evolution he or she has gone through to reach his or her current performance level.

When using the portfolio strategy for online teaching, be sure to involve your learners in selecting what they should include in their portfolios. As the course begins, give your students the criteria you'll be using to evaluate their portfolios.

Make sure the learners self-reflect and self-evaluate their own progress along the way. And be sure the learners date their work!

87. Use performance evaluation.

Performance evaluation involves assessing a skill the learner needs to accomplish a specific task. It's a technique requiring that learners know not only **what** to do, but also **how to do it.**

Performance evaluations usually refer to psychomotor or physical tasks. And so you might (rightly so!) wonder how you might accomplish this task in the online environment. It's not as difficult as you might think. In language courses, for example, learners might record their voices as wave (.wav) files and attach those files to an e-mail or upload them to your conferencing system. The same thing may occur with the recording of movements into a video format.

If you use this evaluation approach, be sure you specifically define what your learners are supposed to do, describe the format of the files they're to create and the materials they'll need to create them, and outline how you'll be measuring learners' performances. Use a performance standard checklist that features a scoring system. You can list the tasks or behaviors that are **not** to be observed on a separate list. Then give the checklist and scoring system to your learners **before** they begin to practice the skill.

88. Use interviews.

Interviews are conducted with one person asking questions and the other person responding. You might think that interviews would be impossible to do online, but that's not the case. You and your learners can conduct interviews with the synchronous feature of conferencing systems by using text-based, video-based, audio-based, or audio- and video-based environments. Some conferencing systems even have the capability of saving the text. But even if your system has no such capacity, you can still copy the text and paste it into a word processing program. Or, you can save it in audio or video format.

To conduct interviews online, you have to develop a set of questions that cover specific objectives. Consider structured questions requiring a specific response or open-ended questions that allow for detailed answers.

89. Use journals.

Journals are records learners keep as they work through an experience. For example, learners in a process-oriented course might go about learning a specific skill that involves them in creating a product, stage by stage. At the end of each stage, learners could write out their thoughts and experiences about what happened during the process.

This type of evaluation promotes self-reflection. It's a good tool to use during the formative stages of students' learning.

90. Use reflective papers.

Reflective papers document participants' learning processes during an online course. At the end of the course, the learners compile cumulative records of their learning experiences.

Here are some elements you might look for (and ask for!) in learners' reflective papers:

- A summary of the common themes covered in the online journals, which the learner has perhaps completed for a module or developmental stage. The learner may include in this summary examples of, or extracts from, the journals.

- An analysis of the participant's learning in the online course. What can the learner do now, and what does he or she know now? If asked to be a co-teacher for the course, what would he or she change about the course content, tasks, and activities? What was the learner's most important realization concerning the process of the course? Why did he or she judge this to be of particular importance? What was the most important skill the learner learned? What was it that was so significant about this skill? What is the chief learning the learner feels he or she needs to undertake the next time a course like this one comes along?

- A reflection on how the participant's experiences as a learner in the course affect his or her own practice. What things has the learner decided to add to his or her practice? And what things is the learner determined to delete from how he or she acts as an educator/administrator/trainer/practitioner as a result of learning about the topic over the last few months?

• Other comments the learner wishes to make about his or her experience in the online course.

91. Use web site development.

With the increased use of the World Wide Web for instruction, it's become common practice to encourage learners to develop web sites to:

• educate a target audience in their field of practice (learning about something)

• perform a task (learning how to do something)

• present facts (which is which?)

• teach concepts/definitions (what is it?)

• show procedures/steps (how do you do it?)

• demonstrate processes/stages (how does it work?)

• provide principles/guidelines (what would an expert do?)

You can evaluate web sites with respect to their content, their design, or both.

92. Use learner participation figures.

During an online course, participation takes on a different meaning. That's why it's helpful to your learners if you define and communicate an approximate number of hours they should be online during the course. You might even assign a minimum number of postings weekly, which will make learners' presence known through substantive contributions to the course, discussions, and learning activities.

93. Use peer assessment.

Since much of the learning that occurs in an interactive online course is done collaboratively, you might want to give your learners the chance to assess each other's contributions to course discussions and common group activities. Such an assessment communicates your expectation of full participation by all class members.

Keep in mind, however, that this type of assessment considers only one source of learners' contributions to the class.

Additionally, when you're reviewing the learner input, it's essential to recognize the subjectivity each individual uses when assessing others. Thus, it's helpful to provide an opportunity for not only numerical rankings but also comments, so that learners' can explain the rationale behind their ratings.

94. Use learner self-assessment.

Self-assessment gives your learners the opportunity to reflect on their own learning and experiences in the class in terms of impacting their grades. It's a great way to uncover the internal journey of each learner. In fact, in some cases this personal journey may be much more significant than you can observe from the outside.

95. Consider how you'll grade assignments.

Grading is a process for assessing learning through tests and assignments. Grading means tailoring the tests or assignments to the learning goals of the course, determining criteria and standards, helping learners gain the skills and knowledge they need, assessing students' learning over time, influencing learners' motivations, giving learners feedback so that they can learn from their mistakes, telling learners about their progress, and using grading outcomes to plan your future teaching methods.

Here are some examples of grading criteria for different online assignments.

96. Develop a way to evaluate group projects.

Ask learners to participate in evaluating group projects. This approach encourages each student to focus primarily on his or her own contributions vs. team members' contributions. However, it also does open up the option for each learner to comment on the learning he or she believes others have experienced.

You can evaluate group projects by asking learners to reflect upon the following elements:

- Learning that occurred
    - Individually generated
    - Team generated
    - Depth of learning
    - Overall

- Presentation style/creativity
    - Organization
    - Aspects of the presentation you would repeat
    - Aspects of the presentation you would do differently

- Content
    - Scope
    - Depth
    - Relevance to the course

97. Develop a way to grade portfolios.

For grading portfolios you might want to use the following criteria:

- *Rationale:* Provide the rationale or purpose of the portfolio.

- *Goals/Intent:* Define the goals or intent of the portfolio, and provide process objectives (what is the learner trying to demonstrate?)

- *Content/Examples:* Use a minimum number of examples that illustrate growth (e.g., samples of online discussions, online journal responses, or resource-sharing comments).

- *Standards:* Assess contributions of varying quality and the learner's review of the progress he or she has made based on a set of criteria.

- *Self-Reflection/Self-Evaluation:* Include a summary of personal experience journals written throughout the weeks of the course.

- *Judgments:* Provide a reflective paper, the project, and the course grade.

- *Organization:* Develop content and displays logically and systematically.

98. Develop a way to grade reflective papers.

You might consider using the following criteria for grading reflective papers:

- *Content:* Fulfill the requirements and be comprehensive.
- *Organization:* Develop content logically and systematically.
- *Clarity:* Write in an easy-to-read style that communicates ideas clearly.
- *Quality of Writing Skills:* Use grammar, spelling, and punctuation correctly.

99. Consider strategies for course improvement.

Strategies you can use to evaluate course improvement include the one-minute assessment, the pretest/post-test approach, the learner tryout, direct observation, asking learners for their reflections, peer review, teacher preview, and your own self-reflection. These techniques can help you focus on the effectiveness of your instruction and assist you in evaluating the (hopefully) continuous improvement of the course.

100. Use a one-minute assessment.

The *one-minute assessment* allows you to ask questions electronically and collect answers anonymously (if you have a program that allows learners to send responses anonymously).

This strategy involves asking learners to respond to a couple of questions to help you evaluate the class. The questions usually go out weekly and focus on actions and moments, not on general impressions.

Here are some examples of questions you might ask:

- What are the most reassuring feelings you have about this class at the end of the week/module/unit?
- What are some questions, concerns, or worries you have about this class at the end of the week/module/unit?

- What's the most important thing you've learned in class this week/module/unit?
- What's the muddiest point still remaining in class this week/module/unit?
- Please write down one thing that you still think needs clarification this week/module/unit.

101. Use a pretest/post-test approach.

Pretests and post-tests assess learners' knowledge and skills before instruction, their growing knowledge and skills during instruction, and what they've learned at the end of instruction. Although this strategy focuses on learners' knowledge and skills, it also provides a direct measure of a unit's/lesson's/module's effectiveness.

You can use the quiz feature in your course management software program or a stand-alone quiz maker to develop pretest and post-test instruments.

102. Use a learner tryout.

This strategy refers to a test run of an instructional activity, approach, medium, or material with a small group of learners before using it for a particular unit/lesson/module. With this approach, you can test your assumptions about the effectiveness of the instructional materials, which helps you find any problems in the materials and fix them before you use them in the real class situation.

103. Use direct observation.

This strategy refers to observing learners as they go through some part of the unit/lesson/module. It usually occurs when learners work in groups or teams. You might have the learners participate in online group discussion to accomplish a project by posting messages regarding their project roles, division of tasks, content contributions, timelines, etc.

By directly observing the group discussions, you're able to gain information about the process of your instruction and the outcomes of the students' learning.

104. Ask learners for their reflections.

This strategy involves participating in synchronous or asynchronous conversations with your learners, individually or in groups. You might, for instance, post questions requiring learners to express their feelings about your instruction (materials, timelines, readings, etc.).

This approach to evaluating instructional effectiveness offers a great opportunity to get learners' perspectives about how well the course materials work and how interesting the materials are. As a result, learners become involved in reflecting on their own learning and what helps them to learn best. Additionally, in using this type of approach, you subtly communicate to the students that you're committed to helping them learn.

105. Conduct peer reviews.

This strategy refers to sharing your instructional materials with a colleague so that he or she can examine a lesson/unit/module, provide comments on its usefulness, and suggest ways to improve it. Having someone else look at your instructional materials helps you identify inaccuracies, inconsistencies, and other potential problems. You usually also gain new insights on the materials.

106. Do a teacher preview.

Occasionally, online courses are prepackaged. This means that the course materials and activities are produced commercially — they're developed by a team of instructional designers and delivered to you, the instructor. If this scenario matches yours, you'll likely need to preview the materials before using them to determine whether you'll use the materials, use part or parts of them, use them with some modification or adaptation, or not use them at all.

107. Reflect on your experiences.

Reflecting on your own experiences over what happened during a lesson/unit/module is a good way to identify the parts of the lesson/unit/module that did or did not work. You might even consider keeping a journal of activities that worked and didn't work so that you can reflect back when the lesson/unit/module is over.

For detailed guidelines on techniques you can use to evaluate learning and instruction, refer to Newby, Stepich, Lehman, and Russell (2000).

Chapter 4

BEGINNING INSTRUCTION IN THE ONLINE COURSE: IMPLEMENTING THE COURSE DESIGN

108. Create a space for learning.

As Parker Palmer notes in the Foreword to this book, the overall goal of any teacher is to create a space where learners can safely explore new territory. To achieve this goal, you must build confidence in your learners so that they feel you're respecting them and taking their needs seriously.

Here are some ways to begin shaping the online learning environment so that you can create the safe learning environment learners need to succeed.

109. Design strategies for assessing learners' characteristics and building learners' self-knowledge.

Just as you must understand yourself as a teacher, it's also essential to understand the characteristics of your learners. You need to be aware that learning styles differ, and that many learners aren't aware of (or have never had the opportunity to reflect upon or discuss) their preferred learning style.

As we noted previously in the section on instructor self-knowledge, there are many tools you can use to help your learners develop greater self-knowledge. You can begin by simply asking your learners, as part of general introductions, to describe how they learn most effectively.

Asking for basic information before the course begins is an excellent way to build your knowledge about the learners in your class. Such a strategy can also give your learners some early ideas about what you find important for them to share in class. You can send your learners questions like these (which were designed primarily for adult professionals participating in a university-level course) in advance, via e-mail, to get the ball rolling:

- Preferred first name?

- Educational background and experience?

- Pursuing a degree at what level, and in what field?

- Current employment, if employed? Years of professional experience?

- Future career goals?

- Learner status (full-time/part-time)?

- Reason(s) for enrolling in this course?

- Goals for the course?

- Preferred learning style? In what ways do you learn most effectively? Please describe.

- Other relevant interesting information? (What would you like to share about yourself to help the teacher and other class members get to know you better?)

110. Design strategies to introduce learners to each other.

In an online environment, learners can post their own biographies and expectations of the course to introduce themselves and to get to know others. They might also offer links to their personal web pages or post photos as part of their introductions.

Some learners, however, may be hesitant to use photographs or other visuals focusing on themselves. Remember that the Internet can be "the great equalizer" by removing the physical traits of a particular learner — traits other people might typically use to judge him or her before having a chance to meet with him or her and discuss ideas and concepts.

Once a learner has introduced himself or herself, it's important for you to respond to him or her and encourage other comments about the introduction so that the learner feels welcome in the environment.

These introductory activities create a "personal knowledge base" among the learners that is a critical precursor to developing a level of trust and confidence within the online environment.

111. Use effective teaching strategies.

Teaching strategies are essential to the quality and value of an online course. When used well and appropriately, they can help you and your learners build community, understand the content, develop skills, and reflect on the online education process. When used poorly or inadequately, however, they can create barriers to learning and discourage participation.

In this section we present several teaching strategies for you to consider for your online course.

112. Gain agreement with the learners about rules, norms, and procedures for discussion — and do so from the start.

Interactive online courses depend on the relationships and trust developed between and among you and the learners. If the learners are to play an active role in developing the course atmosphere, you must **preliminarily** define the structure, rules, norms, and procedures for course discussions upfront — but then give your learners the chance to suggest important modifications.

Some teachers routinely build in and act upon the opportunity for revisions in the course plan and structure. Doing so gives learners a sense of ownership for the community that they're helping create.

113. Use a freeflowing and interactive content and structure.

If you want to engage learners with the course content and with each other, you need to develop a free-flowing, interactive framework around which you can structure the class. Through a more flexible framework, your learners can help pinpoint where they must study the content more deeply and where they have a solid understanding of it and can move more quickly.

Since not all learners are at the same level, the free-flowing nature of the course can also help connect more experienced learners with those who are discovering the information for the first time.

114. Develop team-building activities.

Forming teams is critical to the successful implementation of team-based learning (Hanna and Conceição-Runlee 1999). The criteria for forming teams might focus upon:

- common interests
- common majors
- levels of experience with technology (some learners who know more and some who know less)
- geography (if you want learners to meet face to face outside of class for teamwork)
- topical focus
- professional discipline
- varying disciplines (for cross-disciplinary teams)

Be sure to provide guidelines and expectations for the performance of each team.

You can easily integrate team-building activities into the online teaching and learning environment because they engage learners in establishing and maintaining safe and positive learning environments. They also enable learners to integrate their personal values, beliefs, and attitudes into course experiences; build leadership, facilitation, and problem-solving skills; and apply content in real and imaginative ways to problems or issues that may be personally interesting or challenging to them.

Here are some examples of effective team-building activities.

115. Share biographical information or stories.

Biographies or stories can help foster team building at the beginning of your course. Individual students can learn from one another and understand each other's perspectives. Biography activities might start with you and your learners sharing personal and professional information about yourselves through the development of personal stories.

116. Share course assignments.

Throughout your course, learners might create four- or five-page issue papers related to the course content, and then share those papers with the rest of the group for critique and analysis. This type of team-building activity allows learners to gain access to the experiences, knowledge, and beliefs of other learners, and to contribute to the overall knowledge base of the course.

117. Create a social space.

Create a special environment for socialization where you and your learners can share informal personal accounts, information about social events, and other tidbits that aren't essential to the class itself. You might dub this space the "Student Lounge" or "Café Latte" and set it aside for announcements, casual conversations, meetings, outside seminars, and personal experiences. A social environment will give your learners another informal avenue for establishing personal knowledge of each other's interests and goals for the class and beyond.

118. Involve learners in team projects.

Team projects give learners the opportunity to practice team-building skills, gain leadership and time management skills, and experience real-life situations. When working in teams in the online environment, learners must necessarily set agendas and priorities, identify team roles, manage tasks, think creatively, solve problems as they come up, and collaborate with each other in decision-making activities. These aren't easy tasks to accomplish online. But you can effectively use them if you're careful to provide clear guidelines.

119. Develop asynchronous group discussions.

You can use this type of activity when your course is divided into "topic-centered" modules for which specific readings are assigned. You might, for instance, expect learners to complete reading assignments and participate actively in online discussions at their own scheduled times. Or, during online discussions, you might require learners to respond to questions posed by their classmates, and to review and comment on the responses of others using a web-based conferencing program.

Such online discussions allow learners to articulate some of the main concepts in the readings and other current literature, and extend their knowledge through interaction with other members of the group. We suggest, however, that you keep your discussion groups small, to perhaps no more than five participants, so that learner interactions aren't overwhelming.

Be sure you provide posting guidelines as well. You might even consider giving students assigned roles to play during some of the discussions.

120. Develop challenging problems.

The world is full of complex problems related to every subject. So when you're searching for problems for your learners to discuss, consider using real-life examples but simplifying them to the point where the focus is clear. By dealing with real-life problems, your learners will understand how things fit together in the larger picture, and they'll see the application and worth in the projects they're undertaking.

121. Promote critical thinking.

The Internet is full of resources that may or may not be accurate or even make sense. In order to process and sort the huge amounts of information that fill this "Information Age," learners need to know how to think critically. They need to be able to evaluate the quality of the material they're reviewing and to connect it with other pieces of similar data. They also need to understand the purpose behind communicating this information: Is it to sell something, to change an opinion, or just to inform?

Critical thinking consists of the dynamic reorganization of knowledge in meaningful and usable ways. It involves evaluating, analyzing, and connecting information.

122. Encourage learners to evaluate information.

Encourage your learners to make judgments about something by measuring it against a standard, determining criteria for judging merits or ideas, prioritizing options, recognizing errors in reasoning, and verifying arguments and hypotheses through reality testing.

123. Encourage learners to analyze information.

Involve your learners in recognizing patterns of organization; classifying objects into categories based on common attributes; identifying assumptions (suppositions and beliefs) that underlie positions; identifying central ideas in text, data, or creations; differentiating main ideas from supporting information; and finding sequences or order in organized information.

124. Encourage learners to connect information.

Engage your learners in comparing and contrasting similarities and differences among objects or events. Encourage learners in developing or analyzing an argument, a conclusion, or an inference, and in providing support for their assumptions.

Learners should be able to infer deductively from generalizations or principles to specific instances, develop a theory or principle inductively from data, and identify causal relationships among events and objects to predict possible effects.

For more information on critical thinking, refer to Jonassen (2000).

125. Promote self-regulating learning.

Self-regulating learning refers to learning new cognitive and self-management strategies. An online course requires of learners the ability to manage their time, process information, plan and oversee their resources, and evaluate their own work. Encourage learners to develop their own course goals, negotiate criteria and assignments, and create an environment for independent learning.

126. Build collaborative skills.

Much of the work within an interactive online course is collaborative. Group projects, teamwork, and course discussions all help learners work together and develop collaborative skills.

As your group forms and the learners get to know each other, people will usually take on different roles. These roles will rotate and transform as each learner grows and acquires different proficiencies with the technology and the content. In this way, learners' collaborative skills develop and grow.

127. Create a loose framework for exploring topics.

When designing your online course, use a flexible framework with open-ended questions and topics as a focus, but with enough space for your learners to develop and explore the issues in depth. Interactions through discourse and discussion help learners construct their own meanings and connect content to their personal experiences. If discussions are too structured, there may not be enough space for learners to make those important connections.

128. Create opportunities for learners to teach and to facilitate discussions.

In an interactive classroom, all participants share the roles of learner, teacher, participant, facilitator, moderator, and observer. A useful role for the learners to take on is that of facilitator. Most people learn best by doing or by teaching others what they're learning. Thus, they can learn actively by helping guide and facilitate the group discussion for a while.

129. Add games and fun activities into the learning mix.

The World Wide Web provides a wonderful playground to explore and gain new ideas and insights into almost every conceivable topic. For some variety in your course, and to help your learners discover how to research topics using the web, try doing Internet "scavenger hunts" and then sharing the resources learners discover through an annotated bibliography or a resource list.

130. Use existing software applications creatively.

You can use standardized software programs like Microsoft Office Suite, Claris Works, and Corel Suite to enhance your online course. By offering word processing, presentation, spreadsheet, database, and web features, these programs can give you ways to:

- communicate ideas in a more orderly or graphical way (e.g., information retrieval and processing, multimedia learning and authoring)
- manage information (e.g., budgets, inventory, learners' records, your records)
- conduct research (e.g., data storage, statistical analysis).

You can upload documents quickly to the web so that you can share them with your learners.

Another technique you can use to help your learners identify gaps in their understanding of the content is known as *concept mapping*. Concept mapping is a visual organizational technique used to represent knowledge in graphs so that it can be more easily learned and recalled. Knowledge graphs consist of networks of concepts with nodes (points/vertices) and links (arcs/edges). Nodes correspond to concepts, and links correspond to the relationships among concepts.

You can use concept mapping to generate ideas (e.g., brainstorming), design a complex structure (e.g., a long text, hypermedia, a large web site), communicate complex ideas, promote learning by explicitly integrating new and old knowledge, and assess understanding or diagnose misunderstanding.

Several concept mapping software programs are available, some of which can be installed on a server. Among the programs:

- *Inspiration* (http://www.inspiration.com)
- *MindMan* (http://www.mindman.com)
- *IHMC Cmap* (http://cmap.coginst.uwf.edu)

131. Use case studies.

Case studies can add to an interactive online course by offering a focused example of the topic at hand, which you can then use as a starting point for discussion.

Case studies are similar to using real-life problems, but you can narrow them down to emphasize a specific facet of the case. By understanding how to solve a problem or make a decision through a case, learners may be better able to apply their knowledge to actual experiences in daily life. (Note: At times, you may even want to ask the learners to develop their own case studies for the class, pulling from their own experiences.)

132. Use simulations as opportunities for learning by doing.

Simulations are dynamic, interactive, task-driven exercises that allow learners to experience a concept. They use goal-based scenarios based on real-life situations in which individuals and groups must understand their tasks and successfully interact in order to achieve their objectives.

Simulations focus on "learning by doing" so they can help illustrate abstract processes or be used as team-building exercises. They also create excitement and build cohesion within the online community.

In order to effectively use simulations, be sure to involve your learners in role playing and multiple problem-solving/critical thinking skills.

133. Use external communities, people, and resources to build content knowledge.

Invite outside guest speakers to participate in your online discussions. Or, ask learners to interview people in the community to add a different flavor to the course content.

134. Create opportunities for reflection on the course, technology, content, and process.

To help your learners think about the "big picture" use online journals that require the learners to reflect on the course process. Reflections in online journals may be based upon case studies, self-analysis, self-reflection, critical incidents, or simply communication about learning or the process of learning online. Online reflections can also take the shape of a letter, sent between teacher and learner, relating to activities that have taken place in the class.

135. Help your learners manage information.

With an abundance of text-based resources, managing information becomes an important skill to acquire when learning online. This calls for managing access to resources, academic discourse, information flow, and service arrangements.

Include in your syllabus all of the possible ways learners can access information through Internet hyperlinks or web-based procedures that emphasize certain skills.

136. Encourage substantive feedback from learners — including yourself.

Your responses to learners' comments should be thoughtful and provocative. They should help stimulate continued discussion of a topic, and help the learners make connections with their fellow learners and the other knowledge they've gained.

Telling a learner that his or her comment was "nicely said" or "interesting" isn't enough. Such a general statement leaves the learner with nowhere else to go with the thought. Since open, active discussion is essential in this form of teaching, avoid limiting a learner's thoughts by using closed comments. Instead, use open-ended comments or questions so that other participants react and respond to your remarks. These techniques are important to model and reinforce, especially when the learners are facilitating their own group work.

137. Motivate your learners to participate.

Attrition is a problem in online courses. So it's very important for you to encourage and motivate your learners to participate. Once learners are engaged in the learning community and the course, they're much more likely to complete the course.

138. Give learners roles during discussions.

Assigning roles involves asking the learners to take responsibility for their own learning in a team setting. Roles allow for participation in the discussion from different perspectives by providing support and evaluating group learning.

Rolls can rotate throughout your course, with each learner taking on a different role at different times. Following are a few examples of roles learners may undertake.

139. Make learners facilitators.

As *facilitator*, a learner may be responsible for initiating a discussion with one or two questions from the readings. As class members respond to the questions, the facilitator moderates and extends the discussion by posing new questions on issues that arise out of the dialogue. Additionally, the facilitator may refer back to the readings to initiate discussion on another aspect of the topic. Facilitators are responsible for keeping an active and involved discussion going throughout the specified online discussion dates.

140. Make learners process observers.

As *process observer,* a learner monitors the group's dynamics. Process observers are responsible for making sure that everyone is participating in the discussion, that there is an evenness of participation, and that the discussion maintains a collegial and helpful tone. In a sense, the process observer also functions as a parliamentarian, suggesting when discussion is off track and bringing a sense of order and consistency at critical moments. At the end of each discussion (one or two days after the end date), the process observer provides feedback to the group in a short paragraph.

141. Make learners information networkers/summarizers.

The *networker/summarizer's* role is to look for key themes that emerge in the conversation, keeping track of areas of consensus and disagreement among group members. When presenting the summary of the discussion, the networker/summarizer is responsible for tying together the whole discussion and providing the learners with a brief review of the main issues, the key points participants made, and any conclusions to which the group came.

142. Consider online office hours.

When teaching online, you may want to offer online office hours. If the conferencing program you're using provides a chat feature, offer set office hours when learners can meet with you, synchronously, online. During office hours you can answer questions learners might have about course assignments or projects. In doing so, you'll help your learners feel that you're available to provide live assistance and convey your interest in them.

143. Take advantage of opportunities for continuous learning.

As an online instructor with the web as a new resource, you'll probably be highly interested in opportunities to obtain course updates and new learning, for both yourself and your students. Fortunately, these opportunities are abundant online.

New searches yield new information, and the multiple perspectives and approaches learners take in their problem-solving activities and research open up new avenues for future courses.

THE LAST WORD(S)

The realm of online teaching and learning is dynamic and ever changing, with respect to both content and processes, and we're all continuous learners in the best sense. That's why we leave you now with four final tips:

144. Read all you can about online learning!

Whether you subscribe to some online learning-oriented Internet discussion groups, faithfully read the "Information Technology" section of *The Chronicle of Higher Education,* or track down some of the many new books on distance education, be sure to keep up with this developing paradigm!

145. Understand that you're not the only one who feels a little overwhelmed once in a while.

Change happens so quickly in online teaching and learning (and online in general) that it's impossible to keep up with it all. So don't worry if you feel "behind" at times; you probably are — along with the rest of us!

146. Know that sometime, some day, you'll struggle with the technology.

Technology is wonderful, but it can also be temperamental. So be prepared to be disappointed or angered by it someday. It happens, and you'll get through it.

147. Enjoy Yourself!

Online teaching may scare you, at least at first. But it can also be **very** rewarding, especially as you perfect ways to involve your learners in their own learning. So be patient with yourself, with your learners, and with the technology — and have fun!

Postscript

SOME FINAL WORDS

We hope *147 Tips for Teaching Online Groups* has given you a framework for creating positive learning spaces online. We hope it helps you experiment with organizing content and learning activities that meet the multiple goals of your learners, for that is the essence of good teaching in **any** setting.

We're confident — from our own experiences as well as those of many colleagues around the world — that teaching online can be an extremely rewarding and stimulating experience. Our goal in authoring this guide has been to help you think through the conceptual design, organization, implementation, and assessment of what we hope will be a thoroughly positive learning and teaching experience for you.

We hope you'll help us learn as well by giving us some feedback about this book. You can do so by visiting our website at http://www.teambasedlearning.com and completing a few questions we have regarding your experiences teaching online, the ways this guide has been helpful to you, and how we can better respond to the needs of online teachers and learners everywhere.

Thanks for reading!

Appendix A

ONLINE CLASSROOM SOFTWARE

Many software programs and course management systems are available to help you offer effective online course delivery. Here are some examples of such programs:

BlackBoard Course Info: http://www.blackboard.com

Centrinity: http://www.centrinity.com

Click2Learn.com: http://www.click2learn.com

Convene: http://www.convene.com

eCollege.com: http://www.ecollege.com

eduprise.com: http://www.eduprise.com

Embanet: http://www.embanet.com (Note: You'll need a password to access this site.)

IMSeries: http://www.imseries.com

Integrated Virtual Learning Environments (IVLE): http://ivle.nus.edu.sg

IntraLearn: http://www.intralearn.com

Jones Knowledge.com: http://www.e-education.com

Lotus Learning Space: http://www.lotus.com

LUVIT: http://www.luvit.com

Serf: http://serfsoft.com

Symposium: http://www.centra.com/product/index.html

TopClass: http://www.wbtsystems.com

Virtual Campus: http://www.vcampus.com/webuol/index.cfm

Virtual-U: http://www.vlei.com

Web Course in a Box: http://www.madduck.com/ WCBUserConf2000/index.html

WebBoard: http://webboard.oreilly.com

WebCT: http://www.webct.com

WebMentor: http://avilar.adasoft.com/avilar/index.html

If you're new to online teaching and you have no idea about which software program to select, visit the following web site, which provides a comparison of online course delivery software products: http://multimedia.marshall.edu/cit/webct/compare/ comparison.html

Good luck!

Appendix B

ONLINE RESOURCES

The TRACE Center, University of Wisconsin-Madison: http://www.trace.wisc.edu

The World Wide Web Consortium: http://www.w3.org

EASI, Rochester Institute of Technology: http://www.isc.rit.edu/~easi

Bobby Online Test for Web Page Accessibility: http://www.cast.org/bobby

Department of Justice, ADA Home Page: http://www.usdoj.gov/crt/ada/adahom1.htm

Discovery Learning Change Style Indicator: http://www.discoverylearning.net

Keirsey Temperament Sorter: http://keirsey.com

CMI Kingdomality Medieval Vocational Personality Indicator®: http://www.kingdomality.com

Netiquette: http://www.primenet.com/~vez/neti.html

The Core Rules of Netiquette: http://www.albion.com/netiquette/corerules.html

Frequently UNAsked Questions about Web Netiquette: http://www.xmission.com/~emailbox/netiquette.htm

IHMC CMap: http://cmap.coginst.uwf.edu

Bibliography

Berge, Zane L., and Mauri P. Collins, eds. 1995. *Computer-mediated communication and the online classroom.* Vol. 1-3. Cresskill, NJ: Hampton Press.

Bielaczyc, K. and A. Collins. 1999. Learning communities in classrooms: A reconceptualization of educational practice. In *Instructional-design theories and models: A new paradigm of instructional theory,* edited by Charles M. Reigeluth. Vol. II. Mahwah, NJ: Lawrence Erlbaum.

Brooks, Jacqueline Grennon, and Martin G. Brooks. 1993. In *Search of understanding: The case for constructivist classrooms.* Alexandria, VA: Association for Supervision and Curriculum Development.

Brooks, Jacqueline Grennon, Martin G. Brooks, and Association for Supervision and Curriculum Development. 1997. *Constructivism.* Alexandria, VA: Association for Supervision and Curriculum Development.

Buchanan, Elizabeth. 2000. Going the extra mile: Serving distance education students with resources and services. *Syllabus: New Directions in Education Technology* 13(9): 44-47.

Burge, Elizabeth. 1994. Learning in computer conferenced contexts: The learners' perspective. *Journal of Distance Education* 9(1): 19-43.

Chester, Andrea, and Gillian Gwynne. 1998. Online teaching: Encouraging collaboration through anonymity. *Journal of Computer-Mediated Communication (JCMC)* 4(2). Website: http://www.ascusc.org/jcmc/vol4/issue2/chester.html

Conceição-Runlee, S. & Daley, B. *Constructivist learning theory to web-based design: An instructional design approach.* Midwest Research-to-Practice Conference Proceedings. October 1998, Ball State University, Muncie, Indiana. Available at http://www.bsu.edu/teachers/departments/edld/conf/constructionism.html

Davie, Lynn E. 1988. Facilitating adult learning through computer-mediated distance education. *Journal of Distance Education* 3(2): 55-69.

Davie, Lynn E., and Rosalie Wells. 1991. Empowering the learner through computer-mediated communication. *The American Journal of Distance Education* 5(1): 15-23.

Davie, Lynn E, and Robin Inskip. 1992. Fantasy and structure in computer mediated courses. *Journal of Distance Education* 7(2): 31-50.

Draves, William. 2000. *Teaching online.* LERN Books: River Falls, WI.

Duffy, T., and D.H. Jonassen. 1991. Constructivism: New implications for instructional technology. *Educational Technology* 31(5): 7-12.

Eastmond, Daniel V. 1994. Adult distance study through computer conferencing. *Distance Education* 15(1): 128-152.

Fosnot, Catherine T., ed. 1996. *Constructivism: Theory, perspectives, and practice.* New York: Teachers College Press.

Gardner, Howard. 1993. Frames of mind: *The theory of multiple intelligences.* 10th anniversary ed. New York: BasicBooks.

Gunawardena, Charlotte N. 1990. Integrating telecommunications system to reach distance learners. *The American Journal of Distance Education* 4(3): 38-46.

Hanna, Donald E. 2000. Approaches to learning in collegiate classrooms. In *Higher education in an era of digital competition: Choices and challenges,* edited by Donald E. Hanna. Madison, WI: Atwood Publishing.

Hanna, Donald E., ed. 2000. *Higher education in an era of digital competition: Choices and challenges.* Madison, WI: Atwood Publishing.

Hanna, Donald E., and Simone Conceição-Runlee. 1999. Building learning teams through computer-mediated conferencing. *Family Science Review* 12(3): 183-192.

Harasim, Linda M. 1987. Teaching and learning on-line: Issues in computer-mediated graduate courses. *Canadian Journal of Educational Communication* 16(2): 117-135.

Harasim, Linda M. 1990. *Online education: Perspectives on a new environment.* 1st ed. New York: Praeger.

Harasim, Linda M., Starr R. Hiltz, Lucio Teles, and Murray Turoff. 1998. *Learning networks: A field guide to teaching and learning online.* Cambridge, MA: The MIT Press.

Jonassen, David, Mark Davidson, Mauri Collins, John Campbell, and Brenda B. Haag. 1995. Constructivism and computer-mediated communication in distance education. *The American Journal of Distance Education* 9(2): 8-25.

Jonassen, David. 1999. Designing constructivist learning environments. In *Instructional-design theories and models: A new paradigm of instructional theory,* edited by Charles M. Reigeluth. Vol. II. Mahwah, NJ: Lawrence Erlbaum.

Kolb, David A. 1977. *Learning styles inventory: A self description of preferred learning mode.* Boston: McBer and Co.

Kolb, David A. 1984. *Experiential learning: Experience as the source of learning and development.* Englewood Cliffs, NJ: Prentice-Hall.

Lambert, Linda, et al. 1995. *The constructivist leader.* New York: Teachers College Press.

Lauzon, Allan C., and George A.B. Moore. 1989. A fourth generation distance education system: Integrating computer-assisted learning and computer conferencing. *The American Journal of Distance Education* 3(1): 38-49.

Lauzon, Allan C. 1992. Integrating computer-based instruction with computer conferencing: An evaluation of a model for designing online education. *The American Journal of Distance Education* 6(2): 32-46.

Lebow, D. 1993. Constructivist values for instructional systems design: Five principles toward a new mindset. *Educational Technology Research and Development* 41(3): 4-16.

McDonald, Janette and Chère C. Gibson. 1998. Interpersonal dynamics and group development in computer conferencing. *The American Journal of Distance Education* 12(1): 7-25.

Mason, Robin, and Anthony Kaye, eds. 1989. *Mindweave: Communication, computers and distance education.* New York: Pergamon Press.

National Telecommunications and Information Administration. 1998. *Falling through the Net II: New data on the digital divide.* National Telecommunications and Information Administration. Available: http://www.ntia.doc.gov/ntiahome/net2/falling.html.

Newby, Timothy J., Donald A. Stepich, James Lehman, and James D. Russell. 2000. *Instructional technology for teaching and learning: Designing instruction, integrating computers, and using media.* Englewood Cliffs, NJ: Merrill

Palmer, Parker. 1998. *The courage to teach: Exploring the inner landscape of a teacher's life.* San Francisco: Jossey-Bass Publishers.

Phillips, Amy F., and Pamela S. Pease. 1987. Computer conferencing and education: Complementary or contradictory concepts? *The American Journal of Distance Education* 1(2): 44-52.

Phillips, Gerald M., Gerald Santoro, and Scott Kuehn. 1988. The use of computer-mediated communication in training students in group problem-solving and decision-making techniques. *The American Journal of Distance Education* 2(1): 38-51.

Poindexter, Sandra E., and Bonnie S. Heck. 1999. Using the web in your courses: What you do? What should you do? *Control Systems Magazine* 19: 83-92.

Sanchez, Irene, and Charlotte N. Gunawardena. 1998. Understanding and supporting the culturally diverse distance learner. In *Distance learners in higher education: Institutional responses for quality outcomes,* edited by Chère C. Gibson. Madison, WI: Atwood Publishing.

Tallman, John. 2000. Who owns knowledge in a networked world? In *Higher education in an era of digital competition: Choices and challenges,* edited by Donald E. Hanna. Madison, WI: Atwood Publishing.

De Vries, Linda D., Som Naidu., Olugbemiro Jegede, and Betty Collis. 1995. On-line professional staff development: an evaluation study. *Distance Education* 16(1): 157-173.

Wiesenberg, Faye, and Susan Hutton. 1996. Teaching a graduate program using computer-mediated conferencing software. *Journal of Distance Education* 12(1): 83-100.